HOW TO BRAND YOUR EDITING BUSINESS

BUSINESS SKILLS FOR EDITORS: 4

Louise Harnby

ISBN: 9798666070642

CONTENTS

1. Introduction: Why branding matters

Overview

This guide shows you how to build an editorial brand identity that makes you stand out from the crowd – one that's infused with the flavour of you.

Once you know how to put the *youness* into your business you can spend less time bragging about yourself and more time showing your ideal clients how you can solve their problems. And what potential customer won't like that?

Branding is a journey. I didn't implement my own guidance in one go – it was a process that took several months, and I'm still making the odd change here and there.

And that's the thing – as our businesses develop, we can gently tweak to enrich an existing message, or even shift the story we tell because we want to move in a new direction.

With a foundational branding framework in place, it becomes easier to make those changes purposefully. That saves us time and empowers us to move forward without fear.

What is a 'brand'?

Many people think of a brand as being an identifying mark of some sort – like a logo or name. This guide moves away from that type of thinking. In fact, a name or a logo is an important form of brand communication but it's not the headline definition.

Instead, think of your brand as what others *feel* about you.

Pro marketers Andrew and Pete have this to say (*Content Mavericks* (pp. 36–40):

> 'A "brand" is the gut feeling that people get when working with you. [...] By allowing more of yourself and your company values into your brand and displaying them throughout everything you do, the quicker this will work to resonate with and attract the type of clients/customers you want to work with – and repel the rest.'

> 'A brand is essentially what people say about you when you're not in the room. This means you can never control your brand because it's what others *think* and *feel* it is, not

what you *say* it is. [...] but you can influence it with consistent messaging across all communications.'

The influencing comes in the form of a brand **identity**.

Emotions versus logic

Emotions are hugely important because without them we find it difficult to make even seemingly simple decisions.

Want some figures? The internet is awash with the message that 80% of decision-making is emotional and 20% logical. However, of the 30+ articles I read, none cited any studies offering empirical evidence, so I'm reluctant to throw those figures around carelessly. I suspect that some clever marketers decided to take some neuroscience research and blend it with the Pareto principle!

So instead of focusing on stats, let's look at that neuroscience research. Antonio Damasio found that people who'd experienced brain damage that left them *able* to function well intellectually but *unable* to experience emotions were severely incapacitated when it came to decision-making (see Ed Batista and Jim Camp, citing Damasio).

Furthermore, Damasio theorized that the brain's emotional processing happens seconds before the reasoning, acting as a kind of filtering, assisting 'the deliberation by highlighting some options and eliminating them rapidly from subsequent consideration ... Think of it as a biasing device' (Damasio, pp. 173–5).

If he's right, in effect, we've already done a big chunk of any decision-making using our emotions before the processing of logic has even begun.

And so, given that your potential clients must *decide* which editor to hire, you're more likely to be chosen if you trigger the right emotions first.

Here's an example:

- If the home page of your website puts your qualifications, awards and years of experience – in other words, lots of factual information – front and centre, you're appealing to **logic**. *Hire me because it makes sense. I've done this, and that, and the other, and I'm the best editor in the world.*
- If, however, that page features a message that gets under the client's skin and makes them feel something – for example, a sense of hope that by being edited by you they're more likely to succeed in getting their first article accepted into a peer-reviewed

journal – you're appealing to **emotion**. *Hire me because I've got your back and can help make your academic dream come true.*

Notice that in the first example the focus is on the **editor** and their **achievements**. In the second example the focus is on the **client** and the **benefits** they will reap.

Why 'any old editor' is a weak message

Put yourself in your client's shoes – imagine them saying, 'The article I'm submitting to the *Journal of Microbiology* needs checking. If it's not up to scratch my submission could be rejected. This is a big deal for my academic career so I need to get it right. Better hire an editor. Any old editor will do.' Not likely, is it?

They're more likely to pick an editor whose science specialism, understanding of the reputational power of academic publishing, and passion for supporting scholars glows from every pixel of their website ... someone who makes them think, *That editor gets me and my problems. They seem to understand how important this is to me and what it could mean for my career. I really hope they're available!*

That emotion plays a pivotal role in decision-making is good news for editorial business owners because it's difficult to stand out when you're competing on logic.

Think about how many other editors offer the same services, have similar qualifications, and have done similar training courses to you. There are lots, I suspect. I know a ton of editors who specialize in fiction editing, have a degree, and studied with the Publishing Training Centre. None of those things will have my potential clients itching to hit the contact button because I'm so different.

If, instead, you can nudge a client into experiencing certain emotions or gut feelings when they land on your home page, you're helping them to decide. You're moving them away from the 'any old editor' message.

Case study – sealing the deal

Even when a potential client has made contact and asked you to quote, a strong brand identity will work for you. Here's a lovely case study from an editorial colleague who got in touch with me to let me know how well an emotion-based problem-solving approach had worked for her:

'I closed a lucrative deal because a man writing a memoir had sections that his wife did not want him to share. I explained how I could flag those sections and suggest alternative content, or how he might consider writing under a pseudonym. He was so pleased that I'd gone the extra mile. And he signed on. I have used your approach and it has really contributed to the growth of my business. I am booked through to December with excellent, lucrative work from very prolific and nice clients who pay in advance. Their work is of higher quality than some of my earlier projects.'

What's important here is that the editor isn't just treating the quotation process as an opportunity to give a price. They're using it to evoke emotion.

It's great brand practice. I don't know exactly what the client said or thought when the phone call ended, but it was probably something on the lines of 'This editor really gets me and is sympathetic to what I'm trying to achieve and where the sticking points are. This memoir is personal, and I feel I can trust this person with it.'

This editor has actively built the solution-offering approach into their brand identity and it's paying off.

Remember, you're not trying to persuade clients that you're the most highly qualified editor on the planet. Instead, you need to trigger emotional responses. If you're a fiction editor, for example, these might include:

- Making the client feel safe, reassured or less anxious because you've communicated that beginners are welcome in your editing studio.
- Making them believe that you and they share fundamental values because you've communicated your passion and respect for self-publishing, indie authorship and the right for anyone, whatever stage of the journey they're on, to write and publish.
- Making them experience a sense of hope and excitement because you've communicated an understanding of their end goal, and how working with you will help them achieve that.

Those emotional responses are what branding is all about. I'm not suggesting you should focus only on emotion, but rather that the factual information you include should be infused with emotional nudges that reinforce it.

Digital marketer Ryan Deiss frames this idea in terms of 'before' and 'after' states:

'Average marketers only articulate what a customer will HAVE if they purchase their product or service. Great marketers speak to how a customer will FEEL, how their AVERAGE DAY will change and how their STATUS will elevate.'

The size of the market

Consider also the size of the market.

- If you're no different to anyone else in a tiny market, you're playing the **supply-and-demand game**.
- If you're no different to anyone else in a medium-sized market, you're playing the **lucky-dip game**.
- If you're no different to anyone else in a global market, you're playing **no game** because you're indistinguishable at best, invisible at worst.

When you create a strong brand that's infused with the flavour of you, the size of the market becomes less relevant because you're not competing on the basis of logic; you're competing on the basis of the emotions you can evoke.

Show don't tell

Many of you will be familiar with the phrase 'Show, don't tell', especially those who work with fiction. It works beautifully for branding. For example:

- Showing a client how professional you are is far more convincing than telling them.
- Showing a client that you're sensitive and approachable is far more impactful than telling them.
- Showing a client that you're experienced has more of a wallop than telling them.

Strong branding is all about the showing, such that other people feel it in their bones.

Most editors' websites don't show; they tell. And the telling is me-me-me – their experience, their qualifications, their training. If you can use your brand identity to embed the essence of your *youness* into your website – so that you make the client *feel* the me-me-me – the telling can be about the client, their problems, and how you're ready to solve them. That's a far more exciting proposition.

Jim Camp explains this in a somewhat combative tone, but the point is well made:

> 'You don't tell your opponent what to think or what's best. You help them discover for themselves what feels right and best and most advantageous to them. Their ultimate decision is based on self-interest. That's emotional. I want this. This is good for me and my side.'

The decision not to get in touch

Of course, branding might mean the decision doesn't go your way. You might trigger emotions in certain people that put them off. Is that a bad thing? I don't think so, and for two reasons:

- Branding is about pulling in more of the good-fit clients so you don't need to work with the bad-fit ones.
- A potential client might not be ready to get in touch now, but could be sometime in the future when certain conditions have been met. If the right emotions have been triggered, you'll still be top of mind.

Andrew and Pete (*Content Mavericks*, pp. 36–7) argue that a brand that tries to make everyone happy will be so diluted as to attract no one. In other words, bland. On the flip side, a brand that resonates with your core audience – your best-fit clients – will work harder for you because it will compel the right people to get in touch with you, commission you, and tell other people about you.

Building a brand identity

I'll show you how to build a strong and coherent brand identity so that you can create those emotion-triggering messages that will nudge the right clients towards that elusive gut feeling … or, put another way, make them feel what you want them to feel.

A brand identity will enable you to draw in exactly the kind of people you want to edit for, and repel those you don't.

This framework focuses on the following components:

1. The profile of the **anti-you** – the editor you are not, and never want to be. I call this the monster!

2. The profile of your **ideal client** – the client you want to attract and would love to work for. I call this the angel.

3. The profile of **you** – the principles that underpin you and your editing business

Once you know what each of the elements looks like you can craft a set of **brand values** that are present at every touchpoint of your business.

These can be used to inform your brand **mission, visuals** and **voice**. The whole kaboodle is your personal **brand identity**.

During my own branding journey, I found that these elements were not distinct – each one informed the other. And so while we'll look at each on its own, we'll complete the process by bringing them all together.

Why you should bother #1: Retaining control

There are other benefits aside from hooking your ideal clients. Recall how I said that a brand is what others feel when they think about you – what they might say about you when you're not in the room.

If you haven't worked on crafting a brand identity, you're putting the control in everyone else's hands. You're letting them decide what your business values are, what makes you tick, and who you're passionate about working with. Do you really want all that power to rest elsewhere? Do you want other people deciding what your *youness* looks, sounds and feels like?

By building a brand identity, you take control and nudge people in the right direction so that the gut feeling they experience is something you've crafted. You become the whittler rather than the wood, and your clients are more likely to feel what you want them to feel.

Why you should bother #2: Making life easier

Crafting an editorial brand identity might seem like an awful lot of work but it will save you time, I promise. Doing the work now means you'll avoid having to make myriad tiny decisions later.

The brand-identity framework will help you make quicker decisions about the following:

- **Visuals:** e.g. logo, colours, fonts
- **Message:** e.g. website copy, social media profiles, emails, queries, editorial reports
- **Voice:** e.g. the language you use and the tone of your message when you're engaging with clients and colleagues
- **Visibility:** e.g. how you'll make people aware of your business across multiple platforms

Why you should bother #3: Brand stickiness

People aren't always ready to hire their editor straight away. It might be an issue of budget or of the project not yet being ready for an editor. Or perhaps the client simply can't decide whom to choose from the thousands of editors available.

If you can find a way to get under the skin of that client and engage with them, you're more likely to be remembered. That's because a strong brand identity makes your business sticky.

What do I mean by *sticky*?

Here's a little personal story. I met my husband when I interviewed him for a job at the publishing company I was working for back in the day. I don't remember what he was wearing or the answer he gave to the first question I asked him. But, years later, how he made me *feel* still sticks in my mind. Fortunately, a colleague was involved in the interviewing process so I let her decide whether we should hire him!

How people make us feel is memorable – sticky. A strong brand works in the same way; it turns us into Forget-me-nots! We can leverage that stickiness – even if we're not hired in the moment, we're increasing the chances of being remembered later.

Regularly creating branded content accelerates the process even more.

For you to do ...

Create a branding workbook where you can record your thoughts and discoveries as you work through the framework in this guide.

2. Profiling a monster (or the editor you are not)

Overview

In the first stage of this brand-identity framework, you're going to build a profile of the editor you are *not*, and never want to be.

On my own branding journey, I tackled this last, but I discovered so much from it that I decided to place it first in this guide.

'I'm not like that!'

Do you ever look at other editors' websites, blog posts, social media engagement, website copy, code of dress, website design, headshots, and client groups, and think: *No – not in a million years*? If so, that's good news because it means you already have a sense of your own brand identity even if you haven't yet found a way to articulate it.

It's not that the way those editors do things is wrong; it's just different.

You can like and respect some of their approaches even if you don't feel they're right for you. Or it could be that you loathe some of those approaches (though I suspect that's rarer).

No matter – thinking about what doesn't float your boat, and why, is worth every minute of your time because for everything you list, the opposite will help you articulate the flavour of *you*.

What does your monster look like?

In reality, it's unlikely that a single person will represent the editor you aren't. Instead, it'll be a combo of the way X does this, the kind of work Y does, the things Z sometimes says on social media, and so on.

To simplify things, pull all those niggles together and create a monster editor who represents the whole lot. Don't forget, all the things your monster does and says needn't necessarily be bad things! They're just not you.

I recommend you create a monster grid where you record all the stuff that makes you feel negative emotions – from 'that's just not me' to 'that makes me really mad!' You'll get the best from this exercise if you're brutally honest.

Here's a snapshot of my monster grid. I decided to highlight key words and phrases that I thought would be useful when thinking about my brand values and mission further down the line:

QUESTIONS	YOUR MONSTER'S CHARACTERISTICS	YOUR RESPONSE TO THESE ATTRIBUTES
How do they dress?	Suits Skimpy clothing	Too formal Unprofessional
What do they say?	'That's wrong' or 'That's incorrect.' 'That's the rule and it can't be broken.' 'Some writers have no business writing.'	Prefer terms such as 'non-standard'. Rules and preferences are not the same thing. Everyone has the right to write.
What do they think?	Those who haven't mastered story craft should keep their work to themselves. Self-publishing is diluting our literary heritage and damaging the English language. Those who haven't mastered standard spelling, grammar and punctuation are less intelligent. There are rules and they must not be broken. Language doesn't change.	Snobbery. Amateur bakers and artists sell their wares. Why not beginner writers? Nonsense. It's inspiring people who've dreamt of publishing but couldn't have 20 years ago. Rubbish! They have skills that I don't, and I wouldn't want to be judged harshly because of that. Rhythm and style need to be respected too. It's changing constantly.
What kind of work do they do?	Edit or proofread for students, businesses, and academics.	I admire and respect this, but these are not the clients I want to attract. I'm a fiction editor.

How do they behave?	Use closed Facebook groups to make fun of awkward phrasing in their clients' books.	Disrespectful, smug, potentially hurtful. Authors use us and trust us to fix these things.
	Turn their noses up at commercial mainstream-published fiction.	They're snobs. I love reading commercial fiction, especially crime, and adore editing it.
	Turn their noses up at self-published fiction. Publishers are necessary gatekeepers.	Literary snobs. I've worked on many amazing stories. Gatekeeping doesn't always equate to quality.
	Are prescriptive.	I prefer descriptivism.
What's their voice?	Moany.	Boring.
	Bossy.	Boring.
	The literary snob.	Boring.
	It's all about me!	It's all about the client!
What's their look?	Blurred holiday snaps on their websites and professional online profiles.	Can't be bothered to make an effort. Might their editing be the same?
	Don't include *any* images of themselves.	Who are they? Can they be trusted?
What's their mission?	To go back to the way publishing was in the 1970s!	I'd be out of work if that happened!

I found this process of monster creation immensely useful for helping me understand what makes me tick, and I think you will too.

If the exercise feels a little brutal, please don't worry. You're on a process of self-discovery, a way of making your business brand exude your *youness*. Knowing what you're not about is just as important as knowing what you *are* about. What others do is right for them. You don't have to like it, but you're not their client so it needn't concern you.

For you to do ...

In your workbook, create a monster grid with your own **monster attributes**. Highlight any keywords and phrases that stand out as useful triggers.

3. Profiling an angel (or the client you would most love to work for)

Now it's time to focus on your ideal client – your angel.

Who are they, what problems do they have before they find you, and what will be the impact of the solutions your offer via your editing services?

The answers to these questions will help you to build an emotion-evoking brand identity that's specific and targeted, rather than bland and aimed at everybody but compelling to no one.

Says Ryan Deiss:

> 'People don't buy products or services ... They buy outcomes.'

If your brand identity makes potential clients feel that you are more likely to deliver their desired outcomes, you're far more likely to be hired.

My friend Jane Wilson really brought this concept home to me when we talked about business branding. Jane owns a couple of holiday cottages in north Norfolk. She's the kind of person who puts her heart and soul into everything she does, no matter whether she's hosting a party or selling a fortnight in one of her cottages. And she always makes it about her guests.

> 'I'm not trying to sell a week in a holiday cottage. I'm trying to sell the creation of wonderful memories ... so that the guest packs up their car at the end of their stay and feels sad to leave ... and that months later they'll still talk about what a lovely time they had. That will make them want to come back ... and tell their friends about the cottage. It's all about the emotions they attach to the experience of their time with us.'

Editors can use this same mindset ... we can think about who our perfect client is and what we want them to feel after they've worked with us. It's time for another grid!

The angel's before/after grid

Now you're going to create another grid. In this one, you're required to answer questions that help you build a picture of your angel. What makes it stand out is that it focuses on emotions rather than logic, and outcomes rather than services, just like Deiss and my pal Jane recommend. That helps you get under the skin of your clients.

- The 'before' stage is the discontent experienced as a result of problems.
- The 'after' stage is the contentment experienced once those problems have been solved.

I've tweaked Deiss's original grid to make it specific to the editing community. Below is a filled-in example based on my own branding journey so you can see how it works.

IDEAL CLIENT GROUP: INDIE AUTHORS		
	Before-editing stage	After-editing stage
What does your client have?	A thriller that no one else has laid eyes on, and a dream of publishing that book.	A thriller that's ready for readers, ready to be published!
How does your client feel?	Anxious that readers will leave poor reviews on Amazon because of repetition, wordiness, grammar problems, poor dialogue punctuation. Frustrated because they know the book needs more work	Excited about finally making the book public, knowing they've invested in the right kind of professional help for the project. Relieved that they've found a trusted team member who can solve the problems

	but don't have the time or skills to smooth and polish and take it to the next level. Embarrassed because they're a first-time novelist who's had no feedback on their writing skills.	they can't, which lets them focus on what they do best – crafting stories. Confident because the editor was sensitive, mindful and gentle when dealing weaknesses, and encouraging with regard to strengths.
What does your client's average day look like?	They're a busy professional with a full-time demanding day job. Writing is often done late in the evening when the rest of the family's gone to bed. What was a dream has become a chore that adds to stress rather than alleviating it.	Their working day remains unchanged, but writing is once more a pleasure and stress-reliever.
What is your client's status?	Amateur first-time writer.	Empowered emerging author.

I've highlighted words and phrases. These highlights are useful triggers when it comes to working on your personal brand values, your mission statement, and your brand message – not just the words you use but the voice and images too.

You can add more information to your angel's bio if you think it will help you understand them better. I gave mine a name and a gender (he's called Simon and he's in this mid-40s) because it helped me visualize him more easily.

Simon sits invisibly on my shoulder when I'm creating web copy, writing queries during editing jobs, creating editorial reports, blogging, and responding to requests to quote. If he wouldn't like what I'm doing or saying, I need to rethink it. In other words, Simon helps to keep me on-brand.

More detailed pen portraits

Some people go even deeper, creating full histories – or pen portraits. These might include the client's day job, detailed information about the other members of their family, where they were educated, what their hobbies are. Do you need to go that deep? It depends.

Those who work on fiction are used to immersing themselves in made-up worlds and the characters who move around in them. If that's you, you might find that understanding your angel's problems and emotional states (the 'before-editing' stage) comes easier and quicker to you.

If you edit primarily for businesses or you work on dry academic material, digging deeper into your angel's life might be necessary.

I didn't create a pen portrait. That Simon is a busy professional who spends his leisure time with the people he loves and on writing, and that the latter has become a frustration – that's what I'm interested in, not what his children's names are or where he went to uni. However, if I'd only been able to discover his frustrations by thinking deeply about his family, creating a pen portrait would have been a good use of my time.

John Espirian offers some excellent advice in 'Pen portraits – understanding your ideal audience'.

Do whatever you need to do to understand your angel's problems and emotions. If a pen portrait will help, go for it.

More on client problems

Some of you will have gut instincts about what your clients' problems are, and how those might make them feel, which will help you fill in the 'before-editing' column in the grid.

I know that some first-time authors are nervous about working with an editor, that bringing a book to market has been their long-time dream, and that navigating the self-publishing process is time-consuming and daunting. I know this because my clients have told me. And if my clients have told me that, it's reasonable to assume that many others feel the same way. The same will apply to your target client group.

If you have established relationships with clients but you're not sure how they felt in the before-editing stage (other than that they wanted to find an editor), or what a difference it's made to find an editor they trust, consider asking them. There's no harm in explaining that you're keen to find more clients exactly like them and want to ensure you're sending out the right message.

If you're a completely new entrant to the editing field and you don't know what your target clients are worried about, there are tools you can use to give you insights into the kinds of problems people are seeking solutions to.

I'd caution against just asking colleagues the answers to these questions in the first instance. Do the research yourself. Remember, you're not building a brand identity for your colleagues but for yourself, and you want it to be distinctive rather than following in the footsteps of what other editors have done.

Furthermore, your colleagues might have interpreted their core clients' problems (and their impact) differently or in ways that are not relevant to your brand values and business mission.

Good marketing takes effort, and too many editors head for editorial Facebook groups rather than trying to learn the answers through reading and research.

Branding is about self-discovery to a degree, and if the answers are spoonfed to you, you're less likely to be emotionally invested in your own message. And if you're not emotionally invested, why would a potential client be?

Instead, try the following:

- Keywords Everywhere
- Answer the Public
- Special-interest Facebook groups where your core clients are hanging out
- Professional forums in which your core clients are engaging
- Quora
- LinkedIn newsfeed posts from the type of clients you want to work with

Client baselines

Profiling your angel is useful because it helps you craft a message that will attract them. That does *not* mean you can't work for people who don't quite fit the mould! You can. My angel is a man, but of course I accept work from women!

If you're filling gaps in your schedule while you're making yourself visible, or you attract a client who's rather different from your angel and you really want to work with them, do so. The point of creating an angel profile is to keep your message focused on what your aiming for, not what is necessarily the current state of play.

That said, it's worth bearing in mind some baselines.

POOR-FIT CLIENTS ...	ANGELS ...
Book you and cancel later, leaving you with unexpected gaps in your schedule that you could have filled with angels.	Wouldn't dream of cancelling because they're thrilled to have found you, and don't want to work with anyone but you.
Can't afford your prices. If you want to work with a particular client group but your prices are consistently deemed by them to be too high, either they're the wrong type of client, or you're not compelling enough or visible to a subgroup who *are* willing to pay. Something has to change.	Think you are worth the fee you've offered, even if it's higher than some of the other quotes they received.
Consistently send work to you late or breach other agreed terms. They might well respect your editing skills but they don't respect your business ownership or the fact that, like them, you have bills to pay.	Might fall off the wagon once owing to a crisis, but they won't be consistent offenders. And they're likely to offer compensation without your having to ask.
Will try to negotiate the terms midway through a project.	Will respect the decisions that were made at contract stage.

Want their editing done yesterday. It's crisis management, and they're looking for a service not a relationship.	Carry out their search for their perfect editor months in advance so that they can wait if necessary.
Offer you weird things in lieu of paying your full price.	Know that money, not weird stuff, pays the mortgage.
Are focused on price.	Are focused on value.
Contact you about work that is not what you want to do or what you are qualified for.	Already know what they want, or are prepared to be educated by you so that they can make an informed decision as to whether you're the right fit.

To reiterate, it's not that you can't agree to work with people who want a service rather than a relationship, or who are known to deliver their files late; it's that you're aiming for a position whereby your business isn't impaired by those types of clients.

When your brand identity is strong, you are less likely to be let down in terms of money or scheduling because the client has booked you for your *youness* and their belief in your message. Furthermore, you are more likely to be contacted by clients who would benefit from your specialist skills.

For you to do ...

In your workbook, create a grid that details your **angel' before/after profile**. Highlight any keywords and phrases that stand out as useful emotional triggers.

Make notes about your **client baselines**, too. These will help you refine your website headers, copy, and terms and conditions.

If you find yourself consistently being let down in one way or another, you can adjust your message to repel those kinds of people.

4. Profiling yourself (or understanding the flavour of you)

Enough of monsters and angels. Now it's all about you! This is the third element that will enable you to discover your brand values.

You can do the following exercise on your computer if you wish to, but Post-it notes, index cards or slips of paper are easier to move around, so that's what I recommend you use. All will become clear!

Step 1: Discovering *you*

Write key words on your Post-it notes that describe the kind of person you are.

In *Content Mavericks*, Andrew and Pete suggest asking yourself the following questions:

> 'How would you like to be described when you're not in the room?
> What makes you different from your competitors?
> What part of your role to you love doing the most?
> What's the most rewarding feeling you give to others?
> What qualities are you most proud of?
> What do others often say you're really good at?
> What has got you furthest in your career?'

I'd also ask you to be brutally honest and go further. Don't be afraid to **include things that you might perceive as negative or embarrassing**; these can be turned into positives when you're developing your brand values. Some of the things in the image below might chime with you.

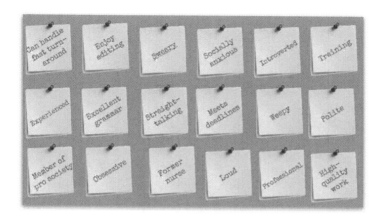

There's no limit to how many you can include. Focus on description rather than quantity. The more you put in, the more you'll learn. And there are no right or wrong answers!

Step 2: Eliminating baseline attributes

Now you're going to start the elimination process!

- If the attribute is a baseline requirement for good practice (e.g. meets deadlines), remove it.
- If the attribute will apply to all or most editors (e.g. professional), remove it.

Why am I asking you to get rid of stuff? Baselines are important but they're not standout. When we rely on them, we risk falling into the 'any old editor' pile.

'Professional', 'qualified', 'polite' and so on are the kinds of things any editor who takes their business seriously would say. It's like trying to sell a gas fire on the basis that it will keep us warm. All gas fires do that. The company bringing a new gas fire to market needs to give the customer a more compelling reason to buy the fire if it's to compete in a market with many other gas fires.

Step 3: Shaping what you stand for

Now shuffle your remaining Post-it notes into **three** piles of related attributes. I'm sharing a snapshot of mine so you can see how it works.

PILE 1	PILE 2	PILE 3
Hand-holder	Not a butcher	Passionate about self-publishing and the opportunities it offers
Like working with beginner authors	Enjoy the mechanics of sentence-level work	Have self-published myself so understand the challenges and benefits
Weepy (adverts, train stations, airports!)	Able to immerse myself in a story	Support the indie author's right to write
Oversensitive/easily hurt	Respectful of author style	Am a crime-fiction geek
Impostor syndrome sufferer		
Cheeky and like a laugh		
Sociable and welcoming		

Having three piles keeps things straightforward. It's easier to remember three brand values, and to incorporate them into every touchpoint of your business. More than that and you risk becoming overwhelmed. Create a brand-values grid so you can record this information.

For you to do ...

In your workbook, make a note of your initial findings regarding your brand values.

5. Pulling it all together: Your brand values

Now you're going to pull together all the work you did in Chapters 2, 3 and 4. Together, you, the monster and the angel will inform your personal brand values.

Knowing your brand values will enable you to create a compelling message (using words and images).

Remember the point about influencing what other people think about you? This is why having a set of brand values is important – they act as what Andrew and Pete call 'your guidelines for consistency':

> 'Brand values are all about how you want people to perceive you. If YOU aren't clear about that, how can anyone else be?'

Adding the monster to your own profile

You've already recorded your own profile in the brand-values grid. Now you're going to add the insights from Chapter 2's monster editor.

Review the monster grid, in particular, anything you highlighted.

Now fit these attributes into the relevant columns. Here's what mine looked like at this stage. The additional information that I gleaned from consulting my monster editor has been added.

Hand-holder	Not a butcher	Passionate about self-publishing and the opportunities it offers
Like working with beginner authors	Enjoy the mechanics of sentence-level work	Have self-published myself so understand the challenges and benefits
Weepy (adverts, train stations, airports!)	Able to immerse myself in a story	Am a crime-fiction geek

Oversensitive/easily hurt	Respectful of author style	Support the indie author's right to write
Impostor syndrome sufferer		Everyone has the right to publish
Cheeky and like a laugh		Gatekeeping is a choice not a rule
Sociable and welcoming		Authors must be respected, regardless of what stage in the journey they're on

Adding the angel

Now it's time to add your ideal client – or angel – into the mix. Look at your before/after angel grid, especially anything you highlighted.

Fit these attributes into the relevant columns. You might need to add in additional rows. However, you might well find that some of the attributes are already in place. For example, my angel profile mentioned first-time authors, but I'd identified my passion for working with them in my own profile.

Recall how I said that embarrassing or uncomfortable personal attributes might be flipped and turned into positives? This is where it happens. For example, in my grid, 'Weepy' has turned into 'Emotionally responsive'. So it turns out that something that I'd perceived as a negative is actually rather good for my business!

So here's what my grid looked like after I'd taken account of my angel's needs and emotions.

Hand-holder	Not a butcher	Passionate about self-publishing and the opportunities it offers
Like working with beginner authors	Enjoy the mechanics of sentence-level work	Have self-published myself so understand

		the challenges and benefits
Weepy (adverts, train stations, airports!) Emotionally responsive to characters and to the author's world	Able to immerse myself in a story	Support the indie author's right to write
Oversensitive/easily hurt Provide reassurance to make the publishing journey easier	Respectful of author style	Am a crime-fiction geek
Impostor syndrome sufferer Safe harbour: Respect for beginner author's nerves since I understand those emotions	Have skills to make a book ready for readers, ready to be published	Everyone has the right to publish
Cheeky and like a laugh Able to put an author at ease		Gatekeeping is a choice not a rule
Sociable and welcoming		Authors must be respected, regardless of what stage in the journey they're on

Naming the brand values

We're at the final stage. It's time to give each column a title that best reflects these groups of attributes. Those titles are your brand values and they will be evident at every touchpoint of your business, from your home page to your email quotations.

Here's how my final grid ended up. My brand values are **professional Labrador, elegant editor** and indie **author advocate**.

You don't have to share the names of your brand values with other people if you don't want to! They're just memorable titles to help you keep track of what you're all about.

BV1: PRO LABRADOR	BV2: ELEGANT EDITOR	BV3: INDIE AUTHOR ADVOCATE
Hand-holder	Not a butcher	Passionate about self-publishing and the opportunities it offers
Like working with beginner authors	Enjoy the mechanics of sentence-level work	Have self-published myself so understand the challenges and benefits
Emotionally responsive to characters and to the author's world	Able to immerse myself in a story	Support the indie author's right to write
Provide reassurance to make the publishing journey easier	Respectful of author style	Am a crime-fiction geek
Safe harbour: respect for beginner author's nerves since I		Everyone has the right to publish

understand those emotions		
Able to put an author at ease	Have skills to make a book ready for readers, ready to be published	Gatekeeping is a choice not a rule
Sociable and welcoming		Authors must be respected, regardless of what stage in the journey they're on

The beauty of brand values is that once you've discovered them you can use them to guide you every time you have a question about your business.

Auditing using brand values

Below are just a few of the questions I asked myself when I was rebranding, and how I answered them with my brand values in mind. They acted as a kind of audit.

What should my colour scheme be?

At the time I was using a bold burgundy. I liked the colour but I didn't think it evoked a sense of warmth or reassurance. I felt it looked a little corporate and lacked soul. I played around with the hue and changed it to a dusty grape colour.

How's my blog content doing?

For years I'd focused my blog content on fellow editors. That still makes sense because I have books and courses that are relevant to that audience. It's also been a tremendous driver of traffic to my website and has SEO benefits.

Still, I hadn't been creating content for my clients to show how passionate I am about helping self-publishers. I began creating blog posts for them, including a series especially for crime writers called Aid and Abet.

Is my engagement on social media on-brand?

Working on my brand values made me much more aware of some of the conversations taking place in closed groups on Facebook. I felt uncomfortable with some of them and decided that watching one's mouth on social media was crucial. I committed to being extra vigilant about my social voice, especially in regard to my target client group.

What should my headshot look like?

My existing headshot was smiley enough but it was greyscale and bland. I needed something that retained the smile but was glossier and more elegant.

I consulted with a photographer and told her my brand values. She believed she could capture two: 'professional Labrador' and 'elegant editor'. She suggested I wear black, and be prepared to put on my glasses to make me look wise and elegant, but playful. She also wanted to subtly capture the stripe in my hair to add warmth to the shot and complement my lipstick. To add to the elegance, she suggested a white background so that my face would be where the viewer's eye was drawn.

Does the home page copy need reworking?

My copy needed a complete rethink. I came across as a jack of all trades, and the focus was all on me. I rewrote it completely, making sure to convey the following:

- I'm a specialist fiction editor, not a jack of all trades.
- I welcome working with first-time authors.
- I specialize in sentence-level editing and have the skills to make a book ready for readers.
- I'm a champion of self-publishing and independent authorship, and have been through the process myself.

For you to do …

What do your brand values tell you about the colour scheme you should choose, the key points to include in your copy, the way you query, the content you should create, the way you conduct yourself on social media and so on? Record this information in your workbook; it will come in useful during the chapters on visuals and voice.

6. Your brand mission: Why you do what you do

Can you articulate **in one sentence** why you do what you do?

We need to lead the way. If we don't know what drives us, what we're passionate about, *why* we do what we do, we can't expect our clients to believe in us. It's about emotion not facts.

Communicating the *why*

In his famous TED Talk 'How great leaders inspire action', Simon Sinek says:

> 'Very, very few people or organizations know why they do what they do. And by "why" I don't mean "to make a profit." That's a result. [...] I mean: What's your purpose? What's your cause? What's your belief? Why does your organization exist? Why do you get out of bed in the morning? And why should anyone care? As a result, the way we think, we act, the way we communicate is from the outside in. [...] But the inspired leaders and the inspired organizations [...] all think, act and communicate from the inside out.'

This is my *old* mission statement:

My mission is to provide an excellent editing and proofreading service.

But this is outside-in thinking. It's uninspiring. It's about *what* I'm offering. It doesn't communicate any emotion or help me articulate *why* the client should want to make a connection with me more than any other editor. Plus, who would want to run a rubbish editing and proofreading business?

Developing an inside-out mission statement

Developing a brand mission is *so* much easier once you know your brand values. It's more than likely that you identified why you do what you do during the process of developing these values.

Recall the before/after exercise that you carried out in Chapter 3. Ryan Deiss suggested we think about outcomes – where we're taking the client, not what product or service we're offering.

Here are a couple of rows from my grid:

IDEAL CLIENT GROUP: INDIE AUTHORS		
	Before-editing stage	After-editing stage
What does your client have?	A thriller that no one else has laid eyes on, and a dream of publishing that book.	A thriller that's ready for readers, ready to be published!
How does your client feel?	Embarrassed because they're a first-time novelist who's had no feedback on their writing skills.	Confident because the editor was sensitive, mindful and gentle when dealing weaknesses, and encouraging with regard to strengths.

When I worked on my own brand mission, the first highlighted phrase in the right-hand column really stood out. It's partly why I do what I do – *to help authors make books ready for readers and achieve their publishing dream, and feel confident about their journey.*

Now think about your monster grid. Does that give you additional clues about where your passion lies and what drives you?

Here's a portion of my monster grid:

QUESTIONS	YOUR MONSTER'S CHARACTERISTICS	YOUR RESPONSE TO THESE ATTRIBUTES
What do they say?	'That's wrong' or 'That's incorrect.'	Prefer terms such as 'non-standard'.

| | 'That's the rule and it can't be broken.' | Rules and preferences are not the same thing. |
| | 'Some writers have no business writing.' | Everyone has the right to write. |

Again, one highlighted phrase really struck me. Belief in *the independent author's right to write* is also what drives me.

Now consider your brand values. How did you summarize your discoveries?

Here's a section of my brand-values table:

BV3: INDIE AUTHOR ADVOCATE
Passionate about self-publishing and the opportunities it offers
Support the indie author's right to write
Everyone has the right to publish
Gatekeeping is a choice not a rule
Authors must be respected, regardless of what stage in the journey they're on

I used these clues to develop the following brand mission statement that describes why I get out of bed in the morning:

My mission is to help anyone who wants to write and publish fiction fulfil that dream with confidence.

What should you do with your mission statement?

You don't need to publish your mission statement on your website. However, if you've nailed your brand values, the essence of it will be visible at multiple touchpoints of your business:

- The kinds of clients you work for
- The services you offer
- The copy on your home page
- The way you query
- How you respond to a request to quote
- The stance you take in conversations about writing, publishing and editing
- How you talk to others about your business

How you talk to others about your business

You've no doubt heard the term 'elevator pitch', so called because it's the story you can tell a potential client during a 20-second ride between floors in an elevator.

Brian Phipps says:

> 'The brand mission should be short and sweet, vital and visceral. It's a way to focus energy, action and innovation within a company, and between a company and its customers.'

Think of your snappy mission statement as an elevator pitch on steroids!

Inspiring yourself

Of course, it can be longer than one sentence, but it'll be more memorable if you can say it in three seconds.

That will be crucial if you're rebranding because you've struggled to acquire or retain clients, or because you're dissatisfied with the kind of work you're doing and want to attract angels. Being able to remind yourself of what your overarching goal is, what you believe in, what you're passionate about, why you do what you do, will give you courage and strength during the transition.

For you to do ...

Reread the notes you made in your monster grid, your angel grid and your brand-values grid. Find the information that's about your passions – the why of your editing business. Use that information to craft an inside-out mission statement about why you care ... why anyone should care.

7. The voice of your brand: Language and mood

The voice of your brand is how you communicate your message, whatever medium you're using:

- **Written:** For example, creating copy for your website, writing a blog article, chatting on social media, emailing a quotation, or querying in a book file.
- **Face to face:** For example, while you're networking at an event.
- **Audio:** For example, being interviewed on a podcast, talking to a client on the phone, or doing a voice-over for a webinar.
- **Video:** For example, doing a face-to-camera for a webinar, creating a welcome video for your home page, or doing a recorded roundtable discussion with a group of editors, or hosting a live Q&A via social media.

It's about language and *mood*. Yes, we're back to emotions!

Why voice is important

Says Melissa Lafsky Wall:

> 'Brand voice isn't just a clever piece of jargon. At the risk of sounding hokey, it's the soul of your brand, articulated onto and within your content. What that soul is, and what it has to say, is up to you – but if it doesn't say something, you'll never separate your brand and your content from the noisy, crowded digital dinner party.'

As editors, we know better than many how what we say and the way we say it affects the way people feel. Even if you've come up with a distinctive set of brand values, they'll be no good to you if they're not evident in how you communicate.

Even though we're comfortable editing other people's writing, creating copy might feel like an uphill struggle. This chapter provides you with triggers that you can use to create your message and deliver it consistently.

Consistency

Aim for **consistency** in the main. If your voice tends towards warmth and handholding and you introduce a sweary rant into your blog or a social media conversation, readers will wonder what's going on! It's not that the topic you're writing about isn't deserving of a sweary, ranty tone, but that it might make you sound like someone else – and that person is different from the one who's trusted by your existing readership.

What elements of your business's brand identity do you want it to convey? Examples might include the following:

- Introspection
- Cheekiness
- Scholarliness
- Brevity and clarity
- Dreamy and emotionally responsive
- Controversy

It's not about right or wrong but about how you want to make people feel and how you'd like to be perceived by those you want to compel.

Case study 1: Kia Thomas

Kia Thomas is a fiction editor who specializes in working with independent writers. Her home page text is cheeky, and designed to put indie authors at ease and make them smile:

> 'Are you looking for an honest, straightforward and friendly-but-professional editor for your contemporary fiction manuscript? Great, I think I know some of those. Let me get you their numbers ...'

She writes with humour and honesty. It's all part of her brand identity and it makes her stand out.

Case study 2: Howard Walwyn

Howard Walwyn provides writing services to the financial sector, and professional and academic bodies. I've met Howard. He's cheeky too, and, like Kia, has a great sense of humour. But that's not part of his business brand:

'High-quality, professional writing, editing and training: I specialise in clear business English and financial services [...] Meticulous. Reliable. Professional.'

He's all about high standards, precision and clarity.

Case study 3: Karen Marston

Karen Marston is a copywriter. Karen and I have never met but she's a really good friend of a really good friend of mine. And I happen to know that Karen is kind, thoughtful, generous ... and lots of other lovely things. But that's not the tone she reserves for her brand.

> 'There are tons of ways to make money from writing. I don't know much about most of them. SORRY. I do know that most of them are pretty bloody hard to get rich from. Hmm. That's probably not what you wanted to hear, is it? Anyway, I do know some useful stuff. I've been making my living by writing things on the internet since 2012 and I'm still not dead, so. That's nice.'

Her business is called Untamed Writing, and that wild element of her brand identity is present in her voice (and the images she uses on her website): firm, honest, amusing, and sometimes controversial.

Case study 4: Louise Harnby

I'm a fiction editor who specializes in working with independent writers. My home page aims to make authors feel that I have their back and can help them prepare for market.

> 'Welcome! Want to make your prose the best it can be? I'm a specialist commercial fiction editor who's passionate about helping independent writers craft novels that are ready for readers.'

I have a sense of humour (like Kia), and I'm a strong advocate of professionalism and business sense (like Howard), and I'm rather sweary (like Karen), but you'd not know it from my website because that's not my voice. I'm all about handholding and sentence-level craft.

The right voice for the right audience

If Howard, Karen, Kia and I switched voices, our brands would no longer make sense. None is better than the other; they're just different. We use voice to differentiate ourselves so that we are compelling to our target clients.

None of us will do well if we try to be all things to all people. Choose a voice that feels right for you, one that will be compelling to those you want to attract. Forget what everyone else is doing. That's literally their business.

Getting the voice right – the brand-voice grid

An effective way of thinking about what you would and wouldn't say is to use a grid (I know – another one!). In it, you record good-fit and bad-fit words, phrases and approaches against each brand value.

It's not an exact science and nothing you include here is set in stone! Go with the flow and see what emerges. Don't worry if there's something you want to include but you're not sure which value to set it against; the brand values act as a trigger only.

You won't necessarily use all the examples from the good-fit column for, say, your website copy. Instead, they might inform your marketing or querying. They could help you choose what to include on your business cards or how to conduct yourself when you're networking on social media.

This is how I approached it.

LOUISE'S BRAND VALUES	DESCRIPTION	GOOD FIT WITH YOUR BRAND VALUES	BAD FIT WITH YOUR BRAND VALUES
1. Professional Labrador	A friendly, playful hand-holder who's professionally trained and experienced.	A welcome. Always sign off with 'best wishes' or something similar. Warm,	Business, formal, straight-talking phrasing. Lots of lists and bullet points rather

		reassuring tone; more prosaic and flowery than businessy, but still professional. Informal language: 'walking in your shoes', 'talk things over', 'have a chat'. I love doing this job; use language that reflects this positivity: solutions rather than moaning. Communicate honesty about what's possible. Perfection not possible/ editing is often subjective.	than explanations with examples. Jokey tone. Emojis, capital letters for emphasis, multiple exclamation marks. Bold promises of perfection and instant success. Marketing-speak. 'Hey, guys'. Over-promising on what I can't deliver.
2. Elegant editor	Someone who edits mindfully and respectfully, rather than butchering the work because of	Use softer encouraging words that reflect the type of editing I do: e.g. 'clarity',	Preachy tone that's prescriptive: 'right', 'wrong'.

	slavish attention to zombie rules.	'smoothing', 'flow', 'crafting'. Use descriptive inclusive language: 'Non-standard' and 'standard'. Keep it clean and kind. I do swear but not on my business website! Use singular 'they' in the main. Use examples from published authors to help writers learn.	There's only one way. Profanity (unless I'm discussing the use of it in writing and editing). Gender-specific language.
3. Indie author advocate	Passionate champion of the indie author's right to write and publish, regardless of what stage of the journey they're on.	Be a cheerleader for self-publishing. Don't be afraid to contradict those who aren't. Acknowledge that editing can be	Preachy tone. Passive voice. Some books shouldn't see the light of day. Poking fun at awkward writing in

		frustrating but that writing is hard. It's all about respecting the journey, pushing forward. But never mock or criticize an author or their writing online, even if they've been a challenge to work with or their work needed a lot of improvement or they've been rude to me. My ideal client is a man in his 40s, so recognize the demographic.	closed social media groups and forums. Slang that my teenage daughter would use.

Your brand voice is something that potential clients hear. However, it's also audible to your colleagues. Given that colleagues are potential referrers, the voice you use in front of them is equally important.

A cautionary note: Your brand in visible spaces

Take care of how you conduct yourself online, even in closed or private spaces such as Facebook groups and professional society forums. Getting it wrong can harm your brand.

Your brand and your colleagues

How would the following statements make you feel if you were the author in question and you were a fly on the wall in the space where these were posted? I've made these up but I see similar examples in closed Facebook groups on a weekly basis.

- 'LOL. My author's just written "[example of confused sentence]". #headdesk'
- '["Example of confused sentence."] WTF? I despair. How do I tell this writer to not give up their day job?'
- 'When you yell at your computer because your author just wrote something so stupid that you have to take a nap so you don't end up writing a really cutting handover report! *That!*'

Disrespected, sad, hurt, disappointed? Okay, so the author isn't a fly on the wall. But consider this:

- We're being paid to fix the problems, not use them as R&R with our editing mates.
- Those so-called closed Facebook groups are not us and two friends sitting around our kitchen table with a cup of coffee. Even some of the smaller groups have 500+ members. Everyone can see our comments. Everyone!
- Are you sure your author won't find out about it? If a group has 500+ members, might someone know someone who knows someone who knows your author?
- Will some of your colleagues decide you're not professional enough to warrant a referral?

Editing, like any job, comes with its frustrations. But a job it is, and just because you can tell 500+ people that you're frustrated doesn't mean you should. Some might find your comments funny and join in the mirth. Some absolutely won't, and if they have work leads to hand out, you won't be on the list.

Review Chapter 4. If you scribbled words such as 'support', 'advocacy', 'respect', 'helpful', 'mindful', 'approachable', 'calm', 'measured' or something similar on your Post-it notes, then using groups and forums to vent and mock is off-brand.

What goes online stays online. And because comments like those made-up examples above are emotional, they're sticky – or memorable.

If you don't want to be remembered by colleagues as 'that editor who's always having a giggle on Facebook about the mess-ups their client has made', frame your queries as requests for solutions, and ditch the hashtags and the weeping emojis.

If you don't need a solution, but fancy using the client's problem as a way to chat, I recommend you find something else to talk about!

Example of good practice

This is a stellar example of how you *should* use your online voice with colleagues in a way that evokes positive emotions in anyone who's reading your post:

A client just asked for resources that will help her avoid repetitive sentence structure.
Do you have any resources you'd suggest that go beyond how to identify repetitive sentence structure?

It frames a problem respectfully, and asks colleagues for solutions. The editor in question is perceived as helpful, understanding and willing to go the extra mile.

Your brand and your clients

Don't use public spaces to tell people you're having a nightmare with a job, that the client has you in tears, that you're struggling to find work, or that you don't know how you're going to pay next month's mortgage. Clients want to know they're in safe hands, not nervous ones.

If you don't want to be remembered by clients as 'that editor who's always moaning about what a terrible time they're having', keep your problems to yourself or talk them through with a friend. This isn't about being inauthentic; it's about being perceived as a professional.

We don't hear Microsoft, Virgin, McDonald's or Apple moaning about how difficult life is – not because the staff members of those businesses don't have problems but because it's off-brand for them to air their damp laundry in public.

Nike's tagline is 'Just do it', not 'Do it if you can but, heck, we're struggling with this!'

Your actual voice – using audio and video

If you have the courage for it, use audio and video to embed your brand voice in your clients' and colleagues' minds. Your actual voice is one of the most distinctive things about you. It shows that you're real.

Think about this: You might have hired a copywriter to create your website copy. Even if you do that, you can still bring authenticity to your written voice by speaking into a mic.

Given how many editing jobs are commissioned via email, you'll stand out if you're one of the small percentage of editors who literally makes their voice heard.

Could you record a 20-second video on your phone that welcomes clients to your website? How about using PowerPoint to create a tutorial with a voice-over? By letting clients hear your voice (and even seeing your face), you're offering something a little more personal – your accent, your enthusiasm, and your smile. And that makes your brand stronger and stickier.

Edit your subtitles

Don't forget to edit your subtitles or closed captions, otherwise you could end up with some unexpected profanity and other nonsense in the auto-generated captions after you've upload to YouTube – what editor and caption specialist Vanessa Wells calls craptions!

Videos are chunky and will slow down your website so I recommend hosting them on YouTube and embedding them in your website rather than uploading direct.

For you to do ...

Open your workbook and fill in your brand-voice grid. Write your brand values in the left-hand column.

Remember, you can tweak as you see fit. The journey of creating a brand identity is one of discovery!

8. The visuals of your brand: What others see

The aesthetics of your brand are the first thing people will see online – before they've read the text on your website, the phone number on your business card, the queries in your editorial reports, the numbers on your invoices, the words in your tweets, or the comments on your LinkedIn posts. That makes them incredibly important.

With branded visuals you'll reap the following benefits:

- Save time
- Make your brand recognizable across different platforms
- Increase trust
- Trigger the emotions you want people to feel

Saving time

I've put time-saving first because I know how time-pressured editors are, and marketing is, for many, something that needs to be done but gets left behind because it's time-consuming. If you create a suite of branded visual templates, life will become easier, and aspects of running your business will be done quicker. Like that? I thought you would!

I used to spend ages wondering about the design of images on my website, whether I should use an ampersand or 'and' in my business name, which font would look nice on a brochure or an invoice, which colours would be most attractive, which picture would be most appropriate for social media.

Once I'd developed a suite of branded images, the questions disappeared.

- I've decided on my brand colours, and they (or opacities of them) are what I use everywhere (social media banners, sharing buttons, website text, invoices, blog images). I don't have to spend time wondering.
- If I need a picture for my home page, or someone asks for one to use on a guest post, or I want to add my face to a thumbnail image on a YouTube video, a booklet or a social media profile, I pick from the headshot palette.

- If I create images in Canva to complement the text in my blog posts, I don't spend time fretting about the pictures; I pick what I like and give them the flavour of me by using my brand colours. I have a few templates set up in Canva and I just copy and amend.
- If I create a box or a section on my website, it can be only one of three colours.
- I have a logo that is styled with an ampersand. I've made a choice and am sticking with it.

It takes me seconds to make decisions about what to include and what it will look like, and only minutes to implement. No fuss, no pondering.

Spend time now on working out what your brand visuals look like so that you never have to do it again.

Being recognizable

Once you've settled on a logo, a colourway, a headshot, and your fonts, you can use them in any space (to the degree that it's customizable).

- If you know me from Twitter but we're not connected on Facebook or LinkedIn, you'll recognize me because it's the same image. I have an unusual surname but if yours is Smith, your recognizable face will make it easy for people to identify you.
- People will be able to take a guess from your colours that a blog image is yours, even if they can't immediately see your name. If I see a red can, I think of Coke. If I see purple chocolate wrapping, I think of Cadbury's. If I see royal blue on a blog-post image, I think of editor and technical writer John Espirian!

Increasing trust

Recognizability is a fast-track to trust. This shouldn't come as a surprise. Who are you more likely to open your front door to? The person you recognize or the stranger? When your colleagues and clients see information from someone they recognize, they're more likely to engage with it.

All the social media platforms and search engines have algorithms that measure engagement in some way or other. The more recognizable you are, the more people will be prepared to engage with you. That means more follows, shares and conversations. And the more of those you receive, the more the social media algorithms will register you as someone who's providing a good user experience on their platforms. They'll reward you with a priority push. By this I mean that these platforms will put your posts, your blog articles, your videos, your tweets, and your business information higher up in the news feeds and search results.

More eyes on you means an increased likelihood of being seen, talked about, receiving referrals, and asked to quote for work.

Branding is therefore good for being found.

Triggering emotions

Images that are aligned to your brand values can trigger emotions in your colleagues and clients – reassurance, relief, gratitude, happiness, motivation, excitement, for example.

The other day, an editor I barely know messaged me:

> 'Thanks for today's motivational post, Louise! Perfect timing, as I'm losing the will to live! [...] Your wonderfully radiant smile has also made a difference! Many thanks!'

Even when potential clients have moved away from the visuals and are focusing on the words you're using, those visuals are still working in the background to reinforce the message.

Think about your home page. You've created a written message that aims to show how you're just the right person to help a potential medical-doctor client achieve their publishing goals (i.e. move to Deiss's 'after' stage). It triggers reassurance in the client.

Next to that text is a headshot of you smiling in front of a bookshelf that boasts *Stedman's Medical Dictionary*, *Gray's Anatomy* and *the AMA Manual of Style*. The smile triggers a feeling of warmth, and the books offer yet more reassurance. Your client thinks you look relaxed and happy in front of those reference books, and that makes them feel relaxed and happy too. That you have those books on your shelf makes them feel confident in your knowledge of the subject matter.

The headshot is visible in the client's peripheral vision as they read, which means you're triggering positive emotions simultaneously using two different methods – text and a picture. It's a double whammy!

Let's look at some of the core visuals.

Headshot

People buy from people, so the saying goes. Using a consistent headshot makes you instantly recognizable, which means people are more likely to engage with you across platforms. Make a connection in one place, and it'll be easier to make connections in others.

But for me, the headshot stands out when it comes to triggering emotional responses, probably the most important of which is: *Phew, that person's real and therefore trustworthy.* That's a big claim, but there's evidence to back it up.

Research by Newman and colleagues in 2012 found that putting a face to words increases the likelihood of those words being believed.

If you want potential clients to believe that you can deliver the solutions to their problems, including a headshot on your home page is a must.

'But I don't like the way I look!'

Don't worry if you don't look like Angelina Jolie or Brad Pitt! If you're injured and call an ambulance, do you care what the paramedic looks like, or are you focused on whether they can get you where you need to be so that your injuries can be attended to? Editors aren't hired for their good looks; they're hired for their ability to do the job. What's important is that clients trust you to deliver what you promise.

Photographs can be chunky in terms of file size. Use a tool like TinyPNG to reduce the size with minimal loss of quality.

There are some tips on what makes a great brand headshot in the kickstarter toolkit.

'I'm too embarrassed'

If publishing a picture of your face makes you feel embarrassed, think about this: If you don't include one, your client won't know it's because you're embarrassed. Instead, they'll wonder if you're actually an agency masking itself as an individual, or they might believe that you're an individual but not who you claim to be.

Therein lies the problem. The emotion behind your inaction doesn't translate correctly in the client's head. It's not perceived as humility, gentleness, or shyness. Instead, there are just holes in the client's understanding; they fill those holes with their own perceptions. This is the opposite of what you want to achieve with a brand identity – control over how the client feels about your business.

Social media

Remember how I said that various elements of building a brand identity would feed into each other? Here's an example of how this happened to me. I decided to invest in professional headshots after I filled out the monster grid in Chapter 2. It struck me that, rightly or wrongly, I considered others less trustworthy and professional if they had a poor-quality photo, or none at all.

Plus, I don't follow people on social media who don't have headshots because I wonder what they're trying to hide. I'm an introverted person and not particularly confident when it comes to putting my face in front of a camera, but I've done it anyway, and I expect to be able to see someone's face if they want to engage with me online.

The profile picture is the first thing people look at when they visit a social media profile. If you have a common name, that alone won't make your brand recognizable or trustworthy. Your face, however, is unique and real, and is therefore an integral part of your brand identity.

Colours

If you don't know your brand colours – perhaps because you've used a theme provided by your website host – identify them. If you don't have any, decide on some!

A colour palette is one of the easiest and quickest ways to bring consistency to all your digital and printed business materials.

- If you want lighter hues, consider changing the opacity rather than the colours themselves.
- Use a hex–RGB converter to keep your brand colours standard across different platforms (e.g. Twitter and my Weebly-hosted blog use hex. Microsoft Office uses RGB). I recommend Yellowpipe because it converts both ways – from hex to RGB, and RGB to hex.

According to brand strategist Talia Wilson:

'85% of shoppers place color as the primary reason for why they buy a product and color increases brand recognition by 80%. People are also said to make subconscious decisions in under 90 seconds, and color is a great way to trigger action.'

If you're struggling to come up with a colour palette, or are unsure of which colours work well together, the **Color Wizard** is a lovely free tool that will help. Place the hex code of your main brand colour in the box, then hit the CALCULATE button. Bingo – the Color Wizard will offer you a palette of similar and contrasting colours.

If you're using a theme but don't know the hex colours, go to your website, right-click on the element with the colour you want to identify and select INSPECT from the menu. A new window will open. You'll see the hex colour listed in the FILTER section.

Think about the emotions that colours might evoke: more muted hues could be soothing, primary colours could be energizing and exciting, and dark colours could add an air of mystery!

Conversioner's Emotional Triggers of Colors will give you some ideas if you're struggling to align colours to your brand values. Don't place too much stock in the science behind this (if there is any). The World Wildlife Fund has a gentle, caring brand that focuses on animal welfare. Its logo is black and white!

Gut feeling will come into play. And since it's *your* gut feeling – your emotions – let that guide you because no one knows you better than you!

Logo

Do you need a logo? I made do without one until I started working on my own brand identity in 2017. I believe it was a good investment – the icing on my brand cake, if you like, and, as with every other brand-visual element, it's saved me time because there are fewer decisions to make.

A logo is unambiguous: the colour(s), words, image(s) and font are defined, which make it an instant and unique identifier of an editor's business.

Marketer Laura Lake says:

> 'Confident branding and a strong branding strategy use design to communicate a message that attracts the target audience you want to entice – a message that creates confidence in your brand while differentiating between you and your competitors.'

Does your logo achieve this? Here's some guidance on ensuring it does:

- Your logo should reflect your brand values. A logo that isn't aligned could weaken your brand by triggering the wrong emotions.
- If you decide to commission a professional designer, and they don't ask what your brand values are, think carefully before you hand over your cash.
- Think about how your logo will stand the test of time. You don't want to be forking out several hundred pounds or dollars every few years.

Below is a selection of editors' logos. How do they make you feel? What attributes do you associate with them? Thinking about this could help you formulate ideas about how to match your own brand values with a logo that makes your clients feel something and tells people something about your business.

Video

Video is all the rage right now. It's popular with the social media algorithms, keeps people on your website for longer, and is underused by editors, which means if you can embrace it you'll stand out.

There are a number of tools you can use – Lumen5, Raw Shorts and MoShow are three. MoShow is my favourite because of its ease of use. Create on-brand images in a tool like Canva and upload them to MoShow (you'll need an iOS device to use this app).

Getting the look right – the brand-visuals grid

As with the voice exercise in the previous chapter, use your brand values as triggers for the mood you want to create with the visual elements of your brand identity.

Here's what my grid looks like:

VISUAL ELEMENT	PROFESSIONAL LABRADOR	ELEGANT EDITOR	INDIE AUTHOR ADVOCATE
Headshot	Huge smile	No background; plain clothes (black) so the focus is on my face.	
Website page banners	Use comforting image behind page titles (blankets, coffee, autumn?) Different image for blog page banner to differentiate it (more fun, playful?)		Clearly identify on home page why indie authors are in the right place: what I offer and who it's for

Logo	Script style; more ornate to give impression of warmth and friendliness	Not girly – don't want it to look overly feminine	
Colours	White background. Three in total: (1) Warm, muted colour to put people at ease. Use for sections, boxes, headers and opaque backgrounds on blog articles (3) Contrasting colour for buttons and additional box shading.	(2) Contrasting charcoal grey: readable and elegant – use mainly for text and headers	
Fonts	Two in total: (1) Swirly but readable font for headers	(2) Readable sans serif font for main text	
Video	Tutorials to aid first-time author handholding Relaxed, informal style to put visitors that show my personality	Services video that summarizes what I offer. Use gentle music and elegant fade-outs	Welcome video to reassure nervous clients (home page)

Size of text and length of paragraphs	Larger font so readers don't have to squint	Keep paragraphs short for readability. Use multiple columns to aid readability.	
Images		To create consistency and recognizability across platforms (website, social media)	To make resource hub attractive and easy to navigate for authors
Boxes	Create boxed 'buckets' of text to highlight key points and themes (home page, services, aesthetics for blog articles) that will grab authors' attention		Use buckets to direct authors to key freebie booklets, blog content and guidance on my resources pages

For you to do ...

Open your workbook. Create and fill in a **brand-visuals grid**. Write your brand values in the left-hand column and then think about how you might best reflect these with colour, fonts, images, a logo, and even music.

9. The visibility of your brand: Creating awareness

Congratulations. You've created a brand identity – a combination of brand values, brand voice and brand visuals that are evident in every aspect of your business.

Now you have to make that brand identity visible.

I'm going to provide an overview of the key ways in which you can create a consistent and recognizable branded presence.

Why marketing is necessary

Every professional editor must do some form of *regular* business promotion if they want to avoid dry spells. What works for me might not be best for you, but we must do it in some form or other.

There are no shortcuts, no easy ways around this. **We have to put the work *in* to take the work *out*.**

The goal is to be in a position whereby your marketing is not what drives the work you'll be doing next month, but the work you'll be doing in the month *a year from now*. In other words, you're building a wait-list.

De-stressing via the wait-list

Strong branding means you attract angel clients. Angel clients don't want to work with any old editor; they want to work with you. And that means they're more likely to be prepared to wait.

As soon as you start engaging with clients who are prepared to wait, your stress levels plummet because you have time and choice on your side.

If you don't yet know where next month's work is coming from, you're more likely to accept the following:

- Projects that don't pay what you want to earn
- Projects that are outside your area of interest
- Projects that aren't a strong fit with your skill set
- Projects offered by clients who make you feel uncomfortable for some reason

When we're desperate, something is better than nothing and we're more likely to compromise or negotiate downwards on price.

However, if you're already focusing on booking clients for six, seven or more months ahead, you get to be picky. You can say no to work that doesn't feel like the very best fit.

And if a particular marketing tactic doesn't seem to be working as well as it did six months ago, you have time to make adjustments.

De-stressing via time saved

One of the reasons why some editors shy away from marketing is because it's perceived as too time-consuming. They want to focus on editing rather than promotion.

That's fine if you're an in-house editor; someone else worries about the marketing. If you're an independent editorial professional, you must wear a business-owning hat first and foremost.

Saying we don't have time for marketing is akin to saying we don't have time for invoicing, or learning how to use a computer, or training to ensure we have the right editing skills. Being fit for editorial business ownership means doing all those things. If we're not prepared to make time to promote your editing business, we're not fit for editorial business ownership.

The good news is that a brand identity saves us time when it comes to marketing.

The most important element of brand awareness is consistency. Your brand identity has given you the tools to do this – a set of values, a voice and a look. And that means there are fewer decisions to make.

- Building a website? You know what colours to use, which headshot to upload, the tone of voice you'll take, and the solutions and outcomes you'll offer via your copy.
- Creating social media profiles? Your brand identity will guide you on an appropriate headline, which headshot to upload, and the colours you'll customize those profiles with (where possible).
- Advertising in a directory? Your headshot is ready and waiting, as are the colours, photos and copy.
- Developing a blog, vlog or podcast? Again, you now know who you're serving, what they're worried about, and what they want to achieve. And you know what colours and images will make that platform consistent with your brand identity, and what solutions the content needs to offer.

Website

If someone tells you it's *not* necessary to have a website, they're not the best person to discuss your business's visibility with. Editorial business owners managed without websites before the internet existed, but they had much less choice. Plus, the world has changed, and so have clients' expectations. The editor with no website has no shop front in which to display their business brand identity front and centre.

Global brand awareness

Having a website means your boundaries are global not local. Take me ... I am no longer a British editor bound to working for UK publishers who control the price, the workflow, and a project's scope.

Your angel clients live all over the world. Help them find you. Google doesn't care as much about where you live as how interesting you are.

Control over your brand

Your website is your single most important promotional asset because it's a space you control. And that means you can ensure your brand identity is evident everywhere. That's not the case on social media, in professional directories, or in advertisements. Those spaces are rented land – they're owned by other businesses who will put their needs first.

Demonstrating authenticity

Some publishers look at websites to verify an editor's credentials before they get in touch. So do professional organizations.

In August 2018, I applied to change my membership of the Alliance of Independent Authors (ALLi) from Author to Partner. The membership controller advised me as follows:

> 'Just to let you know, there are some basics that need to be in place. You will need your website ready and available for evaluation, with your offering and pricing clearly specified. You need to have a proven track record of delivering quality services and testimonials to that effect ... It's not possible for the Watchdog desk to evaluate things otherwise.'

Because everything was in order ALLi confirmed my regrade within two working days. I didn't have to do anything other than give them the URL: 'You've passed with flying colours,' I was told.

It's likely that any professional organization you're seeking an affiliation with will expect you to be able to demonstrate a professional online business space – no matter whether you're a medical, technical, business, academic or fiction editor.

Key things to remember

- Infuse your website with your brand identity so that visitors know they're in the right place and feel good about being there.
- Make your site primarily about the client – offer solutions to their problems rather than bombarding them with you-stuff.
- When you talk about yourself, do it in a way that shows the client you can take them to Deiss's 'after' stage. So instead of saying you edit blog content, say you take the worry away from bloggers by making their content reader-ready. Instead of saying you edit academic journals and books, say you help authors achieve their submission goals. Instead of saying you proofread for non-native-English-speaking students, say you'll make their thesis readable for an assessor. Again, you'll evoke emotion in the client because you're demonstrating a respect for the bigger picture rather than focusing on your services.
- Link to your website every time you're given the opportunity.

Social media

Social media can be a rabbit hole – no doubt about it. Still, it's free and probably used by most of your potential clients to engage with others in their business. Some of those clients might use it to find editors, and that means you should have a branded presence there.

Social media is all about engagement. Use it to do the following and you will build brand awareness:

- Have conversations with colleagues and clients
- Answer questions and help others
- Share your content
- Share other people's content

Being on-brand

Create consistent profiles. Use a headshot and on-brand images so that you're recognizable across different platforms.

Think, too, about your brand voice if you're feeling the need to vent. The spaces may be defined as 'closed' or 'private', but the membership could still be huge, and that means potentially hundreds of people can see – and remember – everything you post there.

Get it wrong and you'll be driving brand awareness, but not in the direction you want. The attributes people associate with you won't be 'warm', 'reassuring', 'helpful', 'educating', 'knowledgeable', 'a font of knowledge', 'funny' or 'sharp'. Instead, they could be 'moany', 'doesn't follow advice', 'disrespectful', 'sympathy-digger', 'taker rather than giver' and so on.

Which platforms to choose

You can't be everywhere all the time. Pick the platforms where your colleagues and clients are hanging out. That will keep you out of the rabbit hole.

For example, editor and B2B copywriter John Espirian focuses on LinkedIn. LinkedIn is where many of his potential business clients engage so it makes sense for him to focus on it.

Post regularly so that you're seen as active and engaged.

Different ways of using social media

There are lots of options for using social media to drive brand awareness. It's about making purposeful choices about what to do and what outcomes you hope to achieve.

Here are some ideas to get you started:

- Answer questions in the groups where your clients are hanging out.
- Create a Pinterest board and pin branded images to it.
- Take a blog post that you've published on your website and upload it natively (i.e. direct to the platform) rather than linking. Do this on Facebook using the Notes function on your Facebook Page. On LinkedIn, use the Publishing tool.
- Create mini summaries of a blog post and pose a question at the end to invite conversations. Use your Facebook Page, your LinkedIn newsfeed, and Twitter threads, for example.
- Create and upload short, sharable videos that summarize your business (using MoShow, Raw Shorts or Lumen5, for example).
- Create and run a chatbot campaign to deliver free booklets or a special offer.

- Go live and host a Q&A.
- Create and upload branded gifs (via Giphy, for example) that say hello and thank you, or that illustrate your business offering.

Directory listings

Directories are a valuable form of business promotion, though relying on them means taking a passive approach. You're playing the waiting game.

Furthermore, not all directories are optimized for the search engines. If you're reliant on them for being found, you're restricting yourself to only those clients who use them to source editors. The market is much bigger, and the more visible you are in it, the more choice you will have.

Still, we'd be daft to ignore them because they are targeted, do generate work and they are usually relatively inexpensive, and sometimes even free.

Visit the websites of broader freelance agencies and online marketplaces, and more specialist editing agencies and directories.

Evaluate whether you're a good fit in terms of specialism, educational background, professional qualifications and experience.

For some, there's no bar to entry; others are selective. Sign up with those that feel right for you.

Use your brand voice to ensure your copy is on point. If you're able to customize the visual display of your listing to pull it in line with your brand visuals, do so. At the very least, use your brand headshot.

Association membership

Join relevant professional associations that are aligned to your business offering. Aside from the fact that you'll have access to networks of editors or potential clients – and all the knowledge they have to offer – you'll benefit from the following:

- The right to advertise in their service directories – **good for being found**
- The right to use your affiliation with those organizations in your marketing materials, especially your website – **good for being trusted**

Consider editing and client-focused associations. For example, I specialize in working with independent authors so it's important to me to be affiliated with the Alliance of Independent Authors (ALLi). I'm also a member of the Chartered Institute of Editing and Proofreading (CIEP) and ACES (The Society for Editing). Both organizations have an international outlook.

Your society memberships will reflect your own specialisms and values.

Content marketing

When you consistently create and deliver content that solves clients' problems you will build a reputation as someone who is passionate about their work, invested in their clients' writing journeys, and trustworthy. You're proving you're prepared to engage.

Think back to what we're trying to achieve with branding. Two people are in a room. One says your name. What do you want the other to say?

- 'Who?'
- 'They seem pretty much like most other editors whose websites I've visited.'

No, I thought not! How about:

- 'She's amazing. She's really passionate about legal editing. Have you seen all her blog posts about OSCOLA citation? They saved my bacon, I can tell you!'
- 'He must live and breathe crime-fiction editing. I've picked up some fantastic writing tips from his vlogs and blogs. I'm not ready for editing yet, but when I am, he's where I'm heading!'

Content helps us show rather than tell that we're passionate about what we do and who we work with. And it focuses the client's attention on our expertise and value first and foremost, rather than on price.

Bear in mind that anyone can set up as a professional editor. There's no one certificate or membership that proves we're trustworthy. We need to find other ways to compel potential clients to get in touch with us, and feel that they're in the steady hands of an invested editor who's worth waiting for.

What to create

Think about your angel clients. What are they writing about and what are their problems?

Here are some additional ideas:

You	Legal editor and proofreader
Client	Law student
Client's problem	Struggles with formatting in-text citations and references according to OSCOLA guidelines
One possible resource	PDF booklet showing examples of how to format every element of the reference
Repurpose	One-page summary cheat sheet – a PDF that can be downloaded from your website

You	B2B editor and proofreader
Client	Business executive
Client's problem	Word documents are formatted inconsistently (think about reports, internal memos and briefings, in-house style guides, conference write-ups)
One possible resource	Comprehensive video tutorial demonstrating how to master Word's styles function
Repurpose	Booklet with the written instructions and screenshots

Key things to remember

- Great content is shareable ... not just by you, but by others. So if you create a useful resource for business writers and share it on Twitter, others might retweet it, meaning it's visible to people outside your network. They might begin to follow you, or visit your website, or subscribe to your blog, or bookmark a page on your site. They might even get in touch to discuss work.

- Your content should look and read like it's from your stable. Use your brand identity to make the journey from shared tweet to website visit appear as seamless as possible. Revisit the palettes I offered in Chapter 8 on brand visuals for ideas about how to make your content consistent.
- If committing to a regular blog, vlog or podcast feels overwhelming, think in ones. Start with one hero resource and place it on your home page. Build from there. The more you have to share, the more likely content marketing will work for you.
- Link to your key resources in other spaces. For example, professional directory listings, your email signature, and your social media profiles.
- Most editors aren't creating content. When you do so, you'll stand out. Clients will say nice things about you when you're not in the room, and that will make your brand stickier.

Build an email list

An email list is an excellent complement to a content marketing strategy. Those who sign up are hand-raisers – they're indicating they're interested in what you offer.

Include a double opt-in to keep your marketing in line with data-protection laws, and make it clear how often and why you will be contacting subscribers. Examples might include:

- To advise them of your new, relevant blog content
- To give them first dibs on spaces in your editing schedule
- To send them a newsletter that features special offers, industry news, or exclusive gifts, and celebrates the publication of books you've edited

Managing your email list

MailChimp, to my knowledge, is the only pro email marketing platform that's free ... to a point. Once you reach the 2,000-subscriber threshold it will cost you, but if you're at the beginning of your email marketing journey it will serve you perfectly well for a number of years.

Your subscription list is likely to grow faster if you include subscription buttons on your site, particularly on a blog.

MailChimp has a set of tools that allow you to customize the layout of your emails. That means you can brand them.

You can capture information to help you understand who your subscribers are. For example, I ask subscribers to tell me whether they're a writer or an editor.

Double opt-in

Mailchimp includes a double opt-in so your list is compliant with the General Data Protection Regulation. That means someone must input their email address to subscribe, and confirm via email that they'd like to go ahead. That's important because there are hefty fines for organizations of any size found to be in contravention of the GDPR.

Emotional post-project marketing

You can reinforce brand awareness when a project is complete too.

There's a veterinary clinic close to where I live. At the baseline, the clinic makes its business profitable by selling healthcare services to owners of small animals. However, it knows that pets are so much more than small animals. They're family members. And when they die, it's heartbreaking.

When a pet has died, they send the owner a card with a handwritten message of condolence and a little packet of seeds – Forget-me-nots – that can be planted near the pet's grave. This condolence package is a mindful way for this business to acknowledge the bereavement, and the emotions experienced by the client. I think it's a lovely touch and reinforces their branding around being 'devoted to your pet's wellbeing'.

We editors can do our own aftercare that will reinforce brand awareness authentically.

Mindful follow-up

Think about your own brand values and your brand mission. What can you do in the post-project stage to reinforce what you stand for?

After an editing project has closed, I send every author a postcard with a handwritten personal message that thanks them for choosing me and tells them how much I enjoyed working on their book.

It was quick to design in Canva because I'd already established my brand colours and font. My brand values and mission statement helped me decide on the strapline. The reverse side features my logo and website URL.

These weren't expensive to produce (I used a well-known online provider of business cards and other marketing materials) and they're not expensive to mail.

My colleague Watanabe of Pikko's House uses video on her Facebook Page to publicly celebrate her authors' new book releases.

The brand-promotion grid

Here's a snapshot of some of the marketing decisions I made to build brand awareness. This will give you ideas about how to fill in your own grid:

MARKETING TACTIC	TOOLS	BRANDING NOTES
Website	Words, images, video, free content, blog Link to it from as many external sources as possible Create content hubs to house blog, podcast, video and ebooklet content Include share buttons on every page (customize with brand colours)	Shout indie author focus from the top Focus on solutions and outcomes – achieving readiness for market Welcome first-time authors Make them feel confident, secure, soothed, respected Colours: soft pink, charcoal grey, and teal highlights
Primary: Blog Secondary: YouTube channel Guesting opportunities: Blogs, vlogs and podcasts	Focus content 50/50 on authors and fellow editors Publish weekly Supplement written content with booklets and video tutorials repurposed from blog	Use brand colours, visuals and voice Use image from headshot suite but one that's more playful Create blog banner with a welcoming, warm image

	Upload videos to resource hub on website	Rename: The Parlour (Proofreader's Parlour no longer reflects my business offering)
	Share author-focused content on Carnival of the Indies	Create a couple of different design templates for use as headers on each post
	Write articles for *Editing Matters* when asked	Repurpose blog-post headers for complementary booklet and video thumbnails
	Submit guest blog to ALLi	Videos: Look as friendly as possible in face-to-cameras. Keep voice gentle and engaging
		All content usable for beginners. Try not to assume existing knowledge
		Don't gate content: Make it accessible without handing over personal data
Social media engagement	Facebook, Twitter, LinkedIn and Pinterest in that order	Ensure all banners and headshots consistent
	Use for distribution of blog and video content	Customize colours where possible
	Use chatbot on Facebook Page to distribute free booklets	Answer questions; never be judgemental
		Don't engage in discussions that poke

	Experiment with text-only posts on LinkedIn	fun at authors' writing in closed FB groups
	Upload videos natively to TW, LI and FB	Take care with venting; save it for 1:1 conversations with trusted editorial friends. If sharing difficult situation, offer a solution too.
	Publish copies of blog posts with new titles natively on LI and FB	
	Post archive blog content on a daily basis	
	Join ALLi FB group	
Directory advertising	Find a Proofreader (for SEO benefits)	Customize where possible with brand colours
	CIEP	Upload videos if possible
	ACES	Include links to website (if allowed)
	AIPP	Use same brand headshot on all
	ALLi	
	Reedsy	
Pro memberships	CIEP, ACES, AIPP, ALLi	To demonstrate indie author advocacy, commitment to international professional editorial standards, and focus on commercial fiction
	Add logos to footer of every website page and sidebar of blog	
Business cards	Use Moo	Keep it simple and elegant
	Take to all events	Use really good quality card so they'll last
	Have some in purse – you never know!	

		Use brand colours Focus on logo, name and URL
Aftercare marketing	Personalized postcard sent through mail, even for international clients	Use brand font and colours Handwritten message to make it personal
Email marketing	Blog subscription list: Automate via MailChimp Include a subscription button at bottom of every blog post	Customize with brand colours Customize default settings in MailChimp from 'We' to 'I'
Events	CIEP annual conference and local-group events Noirwich annual crime lit festival Roundtable invitations Accept invitations to speak as often as possible	CIEP: Friendly, warm, encourage conversation, Noirwich: Incorporate and cite knowledge acquired in blog posts Roundtable: Be smiley, friendly. Emphasize indie author focus and crime specialism

Other ideas

I've not mentioned business cards, sending emails, telephoning and writing letters to prospects, advertising in print and online directories like Yell and Free Index, decals on your car window, attending networking events, joining a chamber of commerce, going to conferences, business events and writing festivals ... not because those things aren't important but because there's already a book about marketing your editing and proofreading business!

What's included here are my recommended tools of choice for brand promotion, chosen because, for the most part, they are good ways of getting lots of eyes on your business regularly. They allow you to move up the ladder and, through continuity of action, build on the successes of the rung that came before.

The focus on online tactics isn't accidental. We have a global market at our fingertips, and the potential to acquire work from clients who would have been inaccessible to us three decades ago. It makes sense to take advantage of that, but to do it well we must avoid looking like 'any old editor'.

The best business promotion strategy is a multifaceted one, where each facet is infused with your *youness*. Use different tools to make your business visible, and make sure that your consistent, recognizable brand identity is visible throughout.

In that way, you can connect with the clients you'd love to work with, knowing you've made them feel that they'd love to work with you.

For you to do ...

In your workbook, record your plans for brand promotion. Which marketing tactics will you use? Which tools will you use with each tactic? And how will you infuse them with your brand identity?

10. Does it work?

Rebranding is one of the scariest things I've ever done! In my case, I wasn't short of work. What I was short of was angel clients. Still, I was worried. Maybe you are too:

- What if those angel clients don't climb on board?
- What if non-ideal clients don't contact you EVER?
- Will there be a net reduction in requests to quote?
- Will there be a higher risk of business famine?

Change comes with risk – there's no doubt about it. Growing our businesses and pointing them in the direction we want them to go takes not a little courage unless we're already in a state of desperation.

Some of you will be struggling to find work. Others will be coasting.

Can I guarantee that if you follow this framework to a tee you will be successful within X months? I cannot. All I can do is share my own experience of branding – the one I implemented upon investing in professional training with two amazing marketers Andrew and Pete. I believe in this method because I have done it and it worked.

I can tell you the following:

- Many more of my angel clients have climbed on board.
- Far fewer poorer-fit clients contact me.
- Requests to quote have remained the same in some months and much higher in others.
- My wait-list has grown from 3 months (2017) to 12 months (2020).
- I do not suffer from business famine. Ever. I turn away and refer more work than I accept.
- The journey is not over. Maintaining brand awareness is embedded into my business's working week. There is the work I do, and the work I do *to get* the work I do.

I'm confident you can achieve the same results if you build a strong brand identity *and* make it discoverable. Happy branding!

References and resources

Alliance of Independent Authors (ALLi):
    https://www.allianceindependentauthors.org/
Andrew and Pete: *Content Mavericks* (2017)
Answer the Public: https://answerthepublic.com/
Association of Independent Publishing Professionals (AIPP):
    http://www.aipponline.org/
Batista, Ed: 'Antonio Damasio on Emotion and Reason' (2011):
    http://www.edbatista.com/2011/07/antonio-damasio-on-emotion-
    and-reason.html
Bitly: Free URL shortener
Blogging for Business Growth (online course): harnby.co/courses
Board of Editors in the Life Sciences (BELS): https://www.bels.org/
Boxshot Lite: 3D-image creation – perfect for booklets:
    https://boxshot.com/3d-pack
Boyles, Claire: 'Why Do You Need A Professional Headshot?':
    https://www.success-matters.com/2013/08/15/why-do-you-need-a-
    professional-headshot/#.W2wuGihKiUl
Camp, Jim: 'Decisions are emotional, not logical: the neuroscience
    behind decision making': https://bigthink.com/experts-
    corner/decisions-are-emotional-not-logical-the-neuroscience-behind-
    decision-making
Canva: Free graphic design tool: https://www.canva.com/
Color Wizard: Tool to help you create a brand-colour palette:
    http://www.colorsontheweb.com/Color-Tools/Color-Wizard
Damasio, Antonio: *Descartes' Error*, Penguin (2005)
Deiss, Ryan: 'Customer value optimization: How to build an
    unstoppable business' (2015):
    https://www.digitalmarketer.com/blog/customer-value-optimization/
Espirian, John: 'Pen portraits – understanding your ideal audience'
    (2016): https://espirian.co.uk/pen-portraits/
Giphy: Free gif-maker: https://giphy.com/
Google Slides: Free document creation and design tool:
    https://www.google.com/slides/about/

Google: 'Check if a site's connection is secure':
    https://support.google.com/chrome/answer/95617?visit_id=1-
    636694112582228640-3843842155&p=ui_security_indicator&rd=1
How to Create an Ebook in Canva: Article by Andrew and Pete:
    https://www.youtube.com/watch?v=cjomXYwevtk
How to market your book and build your author platform using a
    chatbot: Article by Louise Harnby:
    https://www.louiseharnbyproofreader.com/blog/how-to-market-
    your-book-and-build-your-author-platform-using-a-chatbot-part-1-
    facebook-comments
Keywords Everywhere: Free keyword phrase tool:
    https://keywordseverywhere.com/
Lafsky Wall, Melissa: 'Brand voice doesn't mean what you think it
    means, but you still need one':
    https://contently.com/strategist/2015/03/05/brand-voice-doesnt-
    mean-what-you-think-it-means-but-you-still-need-one/
Lake, Laura: 'What Role Does Your Logo Play in Your Brand
    Strategy?' (2018): https://www.thebalancesmb.com/what-role-does-
    your-logo-play-in-your-branding-strategy-2294842
Liflander, Mark: Cited in Harrison: 'Make Sure Your Headshot
    Matches Your Brand', Forbes (2016):
    https://www.forbes.com/sites/kateharrison/2016/04/14/how-to-
    make-sure-your-headshot-matches-your-brand/#1d33defa4d41
List of national editorial societies (worldwide):
    https://www.louiseharnbyproofreader.com/editing--proofreading-
    societies.html
Lumen5: Free video creation tool: https://lumen5.com/
MailChimp: Email marketing distribution: https://mailchimp.com/
Marketing Your Editing & Proofreading Business: Book by Louise
    Harnby: harnby.co/books
MoShow: Video creation app available via Google Apps and Apple
    stores: https://moshowapp.com/
Newman E.J., Garry, M., Bernstein, D.M., Kantner, J., and Lindsay,
    D.S. (2012). 'Nonprobative photographs (or words) inflate
    truthiness', Psychonomic Bulletin and Review, 19(5): 969–74
Omnibus: Editorial Business Planning and Marketing: Book by Louise
    Harnby: harnby.co/books
Pearman, Laura: 'Why your business needs great headshot photography
    (and how to get it)', Janet Murray Podcast (2015):

https://www.janetmurray.co.uk/169-why-your-business-needs-great-headshot-photography-and-how-to-get-it-with-laura-pearman/

Phipps, Brian: 'How to define the brand mission' (2012): http://tenayagroup.com/blog/2008/02/08/how-to-define-the-brand-mission/

Pixabay: Royalty-free images: https://pixabay.com/

Quora: https://www.quora.com/

Sinek, Simon: 'How great leaders inspire action' (TED Talk): https://www.ted.com/talks/simon_sinek_how_great_leaders_inspire_action

Snagit: Snipping, screencasting and image-annotation tool: https://www.techsmith.com/screen-capture.html

The Emotional Triggers of Colours: Tool to assist with colour choice: https://www.conversioner.com/blog/color-psychology

TinyPNG: Image compressor: https://tinypng.com/

Twitter Media Studio – from your Twitter account, click on your small circular profile photo. Choose Media Studio from the dropdown menu

Unsplash: Royalty-free images: https://unsplash.com/

Why No Padlock: Free online tool that locates insecure code and images on your website: https://www.whynopadlock.com/

Wilson, Talia: 'How to increase conversions using color psychology': https://www.conversioner.com/blog/color-psychology

Yellowpipe: Brand-colour converter (hex and RGB): http://www.yellowpipe.com/yis/tools/hex-to-rgb/color-converter.php

Ziglar, Zig: *Secrets of Closing the Sale*, Revell (1984)

Printed in Great Britain
by Amazon